You Never Really Lose

Karah Y. Greene

*To Mom and Dad,
for your unwavering support
and unconditional love*

Table of Contents

Social Work & Advocacy

- Eye Contact
- I can't help but wonder...
- If I had my life to live over
- In a Poor Man's Car
- Puzzle Pieces
- Someone Else
- Where are you, Jesus?
- In Her Shoes
- Curtains and Streetlights
- In Hiding

Surviving
Sexual
Violence

#MeToo

She grabs the paintbrush
and makes a black streak across the blank
canvas.
With a lit cigarette in the other hand,
She dips the brush back into the black
paint,
Sighs, and continues painting black
streaks.
She tells me, "I knew the anger in their
hands before I could
Understand the hands on the clock.
My childhood was gone
Before I even knew what it was.
I was grasping for the door before I could
reach the monkey bar."
I tell her it wasn't her fault.
She takes a drag and continues to paint
black.
"I was praying for a savior before I even
knew about Jesus.
Tell me what I'll say to my lover when he
wants a child.
Tell me what I'll say when people ask
about my scars."
I ask her why people might ask about her
scars.
She rolls up her sleeves,

Numerous white lines streaked across her forearms.
I see black lines on the white canvas
And wonder if that's what she's been trying to tell me
Without having to show me.
She dips the brush in the teal blue,
Starts painting shapes along one of the black streaks.
She says, "Age doesn't apply to me… what does it mean to not know the ache?"
"Do you think I'm addicted to pain?"
I tell her I don't think so.
"I think it's just all you've known.
And I know you're trying your hardest."
She replies with a question, "Do you think anyone will ever understand?"
I look into her eyes,
Solemn and silent,
As she exhales smoke and it lands on the canvas before her,
I notice she's drawn a teal dove,
Sitting on black wire.
I look back at her and softly say,
"I do."
I reach for the paintbrush.
She says she needs a minute and walks outside.
When she returns with another lit cigarette

she sees two doves perched on the black
streak,
A golden sun painted above them.

I'm working on not saying goodbye

My mother has a friend who refuses
to say "bye" at the end of a phone call.
If that were to be the last time
she would ever
talk
to that person,
bye is not the last word she would
want to pass from her lips
into their ears.
They say to never go to bed upset at
someone you love,
To never hang up, out of anger,
In the middle of a conversation.
Two days ago, I hung up on my mother.
I took a shower and could only think of her
friend who never says bye.
My love sometimes forgets
that life is an ocean that
graces the shoreline by
leaving seashells and
taking some away
into the blue endless water.
I sometimes forget that
I'm not the only one feeling something
When I abruptly and angrily hang up on
you.

I spoke to my mother on the phone for
over two hours yesterday
without a single moment of anger or haste.
How grateful I am for second chances,
for a shift in perspective,
for a love that understands that
My love has a temper.
It tends to step on your feet in the middle
of a waltz.

My love sometimes remembers
how my mother and father's love
has carried me back from the trenches of
lost faith.

My love sometimes remembers what it has
forgotten.
That's when I know I am still growing.
That's when I most know that I am loved.
That's when I make phone calls,
and I make sure that there is an "I love
you"
Between the "Hello" and "Bye".
When I remember to love,
I find that I am doing something right.
I will give perpetually,
And everyone will go to bed at night
knowing that they are
Loved.

Forgiveness

In the dark.
Made of the dark.
There is a stillness that comes over me,
And I wonder why the darkness earned a
bad name.
What makes darkness so scary,
So feared?
Sometimes the comfort of not seeing,
Being blind to the monsters
Blind to the wrongdoings
Blind to the hurt
Blind to the ache
-these feelings don't always feel so
negative.
Negatives help you develop
From the empty spaces
Where you were taught nothing could ever
grow.

Sometimes, it is in the darkness where
We are given permission to feel without
fear of judgment.
Wearing our scars,
Uncovering the truths we attempted to
bury.
Forgiveness can sound radical,
But it was never radical to You.

It was a way of Being.
It *is*.
Forgiveness needs no light to develop.
Forgiveness needs no airtime to be
sincere.
Forgiveness needs only to be felt,
In the spaces you thought were empty,
Where you were convinced nothing could
ever grow.

Tangible

My sister covered all four walls of her
bedroom
with photographs of cherished childhood
memories,
moments captured on camera film
smiles
and almost tangible happiness.
When I came forward about the abuse I
suffered
at the hands of these faces in the pictures
She took them down.
Not just the ones that had the abusers.
All of them,
every memory withdrawn from the walls
that rang
of familial love
of untainted bonds
of eyes that held hurricanes
and rainbows in the aftermath.
I had tarnished their identities
My eyes jarred open
Long enough to remember their touch,
Crimson spotting from a bleeding heart.
Fingerprints imprinted on my lungs,
every breath a testament to survival.
My sister taped those pictures to the walls
expecting joy to echo from faces

of a time when her biggest worry was if I would
play pretend with her
of a time when my biggest worry was if I could
conceal the pain long enough to keep a family together.
Together
we overcame the struggle
of recanted dreams
and fake safety nets from guilty embrace
to find ourselves at the edge of all our losses.
We created a new reality
One with almost tangible purity
In the eyes of God
We saw grace and hope
and Love.
Love
the compassionate healing
the forgiveness given to me
from myself
for myself.
I breathe in,
the four walls now bare of any faces
and yet,
I have never felt more loved than I do right
Now.

I am not here

I hear their voices.
They are muffled at this point
Because I am not here.
I am somewhere else,
At my safe place,
Under an oak tree
In the shade
Hidden away from the abrasive sun.
My hair is down,
And I am
Free.
Free.
From their grips
On my ankles,
On my thighs,
On my wrists.
Their hold on my legs as they shove their
manhood inside.
I am free.
There is a breeze in his back yard,
But I cannot feel it.
I hear the chicken coop.
I hear the Florida sun mocking me.
I want to be free.
Am I?
I hear them tell me I am beautiful
And ugly in the same breath.

They do not miss a beat
To tell me this is exactly what I want,
What I need.
Three unholy holes; I am no longer whole.
I've stopped crying at this point.
It has not served a purpose at all
Other than to make them shove harder
And hold tighter.
I wake up and realize this is all a dream.
This is not happening anymore.
I wake up,
And I am here.
And I am free.

Relationships

They tell you that time will make things
more manageable.
And you will know what you want
When he finally walks into your life
When she finally walks into your life.
When things start finally making sense for
you.
But what they do not tell you
Is you won't know what you want right
away.
Maybe things will feel so new at first,
Your heart and mind will feel safe and
okay.
And everything will be great.
But the days pass
And you start thinking more of their faces
-not her face.
And you can't feel anything when she
holds you close.
You can't let yourself feel all of the good
that's happening between the two of you.
And you can't tell her why
Because you don't know why.
Everything was so good
And now everything feels like
Too soon.
Too much.

Too fast.
And you're wondering if this isn't the right time.
Or if you're just not the right person.
It was never right before.
Shouldn't it feel right now?
Shouldn't you be able to feel all the good that's happening
Instead of questioning every touch
And doubting every kiss
And wondering why this has to be so difficult.
Why does this have to be so confusing?
When you've wanted this for so long,
But now you feel like you just can't stop wondering
Why things have to hurt to feel good.
Why you can't just embrace this moment
With her
And you
And it's just you.
She seems fine.
So why aren't you?
Why do you have to do this?
Why can't it be easier?
Why are you still asking yourself these questions,
Instead of letting things
Be?

Will she even understand why you're wired this way?
When you can't even understand it?
Half lovable, half chewed up and spit out ruins.
Nothing makes sense to the person with the lived experience.
How does one make sense of the unsensible?
Maybe you don't.
Maybe you just wait for more time to pass,
To make all of this more manageable.

Shaking Hands

My family sent out a signal that carried its
way through the ocean.
They kept trying to find me,
Shining a spotlight on the murky water.
They held tight to their life vests and dove
in,
Searching for a sign of life.
It was so dark the night they tried to find
me.
They weren't sure they ever would.
But they didn't give up.
They searched
And they searched
And they searched.
I swam so far that I started drowning from
fatigue,
And every second was precious.
I was hypothermic.
See, it was cold in the water,
And I could feel it in my bones
That I was running out of time.
The people who had stayed on the boat
While the others swam in the water to get
a better look
Threw a rope my way.
I still wasn't sure I wanted to be saved.

A person in the water forced me to grab the rope and
Held me up while we were being submerged in darkness.
When they found me
And I came to my senses,
I was shaking
And soaked in regret
For ever trying to swim in the water.
I had voluntarily jumped off the boat,
Into the unforgiving ocean
And I had leapt in knowing I had forgotten how to swim.
I did so anyway,
And when they found me
I caught my breath
And felt the weight of my choice,
Heavy on my chest.

My hands shake constantly now.
At least I am finally back on solid ground.

Unresolved

How can the best part of me find closure
with the worst part of you?
When my bed is empty
And sometimes my heart is, too.
When my two cents were not spoken
And my mercy on you
Feels more like suffering for me.
When my mind is racing
And the clock's hands are slow.
When I am here standing,
And everyone else goes.
When God feels far
And everyone is so distant.
When things happened so gradually
And yet life changed in an instant.

Almost a decade of broken silence,
And I am still sitting here,
Writing my thoughts
Searching for solace
But never finding it.
And all I can ask of myself,
Is why I have never asked you
To live with your sins
The way I have had to live with them.
And I am disheartened to find
That there's only silence on my end, too.

Springtime & Daffodils

I plucked a daffodil from the ground the
other day.
I told my mom to make a wish and blow
the seeds away.
The seeds stayed.
We laughed.
It is early April.
The plants and trees are beginning to
bloom.
Some are still bare,
No leaves.
I think humans are like that.
Some of us are like the daffodil that
refuses to make a
Wish.
Some of us are waiting to get our colors
back
While we watch everyone else's vibrant
streaks highlight the blue sky.
We all want to grow tall as a sycamore
Or bloom like a cherry blossom.
Me,
I want to be neither.
I want to be the earth,
The ground that helps them grow.
But we all know that means I'll get
stepped on.

Maybe that's okay.
It's springtime, and I'm talking about
suicide.
Maybe I'm lying to myself.
Maybe the sycamore and cherry blossoms
have it made.
Maybe I'm forgetting to water my roots.
Maybe I'm drying out.
I wonder,
After all of this,
If I will remember not to step on my own
toes
And to not step on anyone else's.
Pounding the soil into the ground,
Seeing the blooming springtime and feeling
the humid, breezy air.
I wonder,
After all of this,
If I will remember the smell of the flowers
My mom bought me the first day she got
here.
After driving twelve hours nonstop to save
my life,
She bought me six red roses.
I wonder,
After all of this,
If I will remember how badly the thorns
hurt,
If I'll keep touching their barbed stems.

I wonder,
After all of this,
If I will remember how tall sycamores grow
And if I will stand in awe at their height.
Maybe I will remember the color of the
cherry blossoms
And maybe I will highlight the blue sky
with my vibrant colors
Because I'll know
I don't deserve to be stepped on.

We are looking at the same sky

Based on my experiences as a Guardian ad Litem volunteer

Yesterday, I damn near convinced myself
you were in the courtroom with me.
I convinced myself the case manager I was
shadowing had your hands.
I convinced myself the judge had your
voice.
I convinced myself the Program Director
said your name.
I convinced myself you were the picture on
the staircase door of who to never let into
the building.

It's funny how trauma works. You can
convince yourself
Something is true
Someone is you
But he's not.
They're not.
At times, I feel the mercy I bestowed upon
all of you
Is another cross I must carry.
I ask God if any of you have spoken to Him
in a while?
"Are they speaking to You right now, Lord?

Can You listen to all of us at the same
time?
Are you really listening to me?"
And I wonder if I've betrayed the five-
year-old girl
-The six-year-old girl-
-The seven-year-old girl-
-The eight-year-old girl-
-The fourteen-year-old girl-
-The nineteen-year-old girl-
-The twenty-year-old girl-
-The twenty-one-year-old girl-
Who never got her voice?
Am I a hypocrite for telling others to
speak,
When it's something I've never done
And will never do
For myself?
I will be face-to-face with an alleged sex
offender
Next week.
I'm recommending termination of his
parental rights.
I know none of you are this guy.
But for a moment,
I might convince myself the cuffs around
his legs and hands
Are, for a moment,
Around yours.

Maybe Justice can find herself
In the corners of my mind
That only all of you know.
And maybe she can free me
And clean the dirtiest parts of me
The wounds that have not yet healed.
And maybe I can speak
And maybe this won't feel like a
hypocritical position
To advocate for the voiceless
Because then I'll have
A voice.

Disclosure

We are talking about drinking,
How neither of us has a taste for alcohol.
You start describing the time you got really drunk,
That it was once
It never happened again.
You were traveling to a conference,
Talking with a man.
"He kept putting drinks in my face.
Before I knew it, I woke up the next morning
Feeling so tired,
We had slept together.
I came down the elevator,
So relieved I wasn't presenting that day.
All I had to do was listen to other people."

You are 86 years old.
You are a retired English professor,
With refined taste
and humble disposition.
You just described getting raped.
"I told myself I would never let myself do that again."
You don't know,
That you had no choice.
That he gave you no choice.

I dare not break this news to you,
A mind well enough to recall your past
But too aged to do much else with a
realization that you were violated
Than to question how you never
acknowledged this sooner.
A woman with a doctorate degree in
English,
I can't help you find the word for what
happened to you.
I dare not wreck the peace of mind you
hold onto with both hands,
Wrinkled, fragile, and full of wisdom,
Except for what the world refused to wake
up to
In your generation.

The day a woman who is raped can label it
as such
For what it is
For what it was
Can't really be called a victory at all.
But that's where we are
Presently.
Aren't we?

Peace

Silent hour, dark room.
The loudest sound comes from you.
Screaming, "how'd this happen to me?"
How could God let this be?

Pacing back and forth,
The truth you can't ignore.

He will tell them you wanted this.
She will laugh and shake her fists.
Tell me now,
What peace exists outside this place?
When all I see is an angry face?

You will travel far,
You never knew how far you'd go.
Sometimes this life,
In all that's wrong and when nothing's
right,
Can be such a lonely ride.

Loudest night, brightest room.
The fluorescent light shows your wound.
Quiet tears that hit the floor,
You tell yourself, "There must be more."

He will tell them you wanted this.

She will laugh and shake her fists.
Tell me now,
What peace exists outside this place?
When all I see is an angry face?

I was once the angry one,
The easy life, the constant sun.
Till this happened to me,
And God echoed, "let it be."

They will talk of things they don't know.
You'll turn away and make this life your
own.
Sometimes this life,
In all that's wrong and when nothing's
right,
Can be such a lonely ride.

But the peace you find within,
Is how you will survive.

January 17th, 2018

I have concluded that the only way to reduce the shame is to use my voice. It is my hope that another survivor may read what I share and feel less alone.

It was a divine intervention of sorts.
I had gotten sepsis and was recovering.
Your grandmother had accused my parents of stealing one of your belongings.
I'd gotten worn down, with the smoking, and the wintry weather and the isolation and the secrecy.
I'd reached my breaking point.
If there's a God out there, He knew the secrecy wasn't going to be enough.
I needed to get sepsis.
I needed to adopt a dog who was wreaking havoc on our belongings and driving you to give me an ultimatum.
I needed for you to give me an ultimatum.

I needed the smoke to clear,
for my lungs to breathe in more than the rotten fruits of all my labor.
Of the rock bottom we hit together,
When I so willingly softened your fall

On our downward spiral that I was too
ashamed to share with anyone.
The ache of the powerlessness,
The ambivalence towards claiming my life
back,
Of the years when you were at the core of
everything I did.
The strength it took to walk away,
To drive twelve hours back to the home I
was so excited to run away from two years
prior.

How nervous is the woman who is learning
to love herself again,
How painful the growing can be when
you've never had a man love you well.
How scary is accepting the truth that the
love you thought you knew was never
really love at all.
The walking away,
The starting over,
Telling myself I would never let it happen
again,
Only for it to happen again.
Knowing the last time you raped me was
going to be the last time.
The certainty I felt in knowing this very
real weight would be lifted,
That I was going to start again,

Simply because I wanted to,
Even if I didn't know how I would.

The fact that simply wanting to live was
enough for me to walk away from what,
And who –
Had been killing me.

Life
&
Grief

Addicted

Your family tells me how badly you wanted
to die.
Tell me how badly you want to live.
Tell me the last time you recognized
yourself in the mirror.
Tell me if it was a gradual change,
Or did it happen overnight?
Tell me about the times you were only
ever as high as the swing was.
Tell me when the happiest day of your life
was your child's birth.
Tell me when your biggest craving wasn't
illegal.
Tell me when your shame was the size of a
mustard seed.
Your family tells me it grew the size of a
forest.
Tell me when you last heard "I love you"
and believed it.
Tell me when you last ran to a loved one's
arms before running to the drugs.
Tell me the last face you saw before you
overdosed was your son's.
Tell me your feet felt like they didn't need
to carry you anymore

at the exact same time you donned your
angel wings.
Tell me the high in Heaven is better than
anything you felt down here.
Tell me you are no longer chasing it,
Tell me you are healed.
Tell me how the face of God looks so much
like your own,
Like you recognize your best self in His
eyes,
How your mind is at peace because your
soul is, too.
Tell me it doesn't hurt anymore.

I remember when I ran to the blade faster
than I ran to my mother's arms.
I remember when I starved the hate out of
myself, the years I only saw smoke and
red.
I remember how badly I wanted to die.
I know how badly I want to live.
I remember living my life on the outside of
society.
I know I keep going back to the outside,
And how badly I want to bring others back
with me.
God tells me, "Child, don't you know you
can't save anyone? They've got to save
themselves!"

My mind replies, "I know that."
My heart says, "Yeah, but you better
believe I'm still gonna try."

Grief

*Inspired by my grandmother, a person
who often said, "I love you hard."*

I think one of the hardest things about
grief
is the void, the emptiness.
-The space where your laughter used to be
-The ring of the phone when you'd call
-The ding of the social media notification.
How deafening the silence is
No conversations during my morning
coffee.
No good night message as I end my day.
A lot of loved ones have left this world this
year
And a lot of pets
But your leaving
Cuts a little deeper
Aches a little harder
And makes the silence a little louder.

The children I will love who will never meet
you.
The significant other who will never meet
you.
The name I will make for myself
Being your namesake

But never being able to do any more than
to hope that you *know*
-Know the difference I'm making.
-Know the people I'm helping.
-Know the love I'm sharing.
-Know the magnitude of my giving.
-Know the depth of my faith.
-Know the acts of my kindness.
And know that it's all you.
It's because of you.
Loving hard
And giving when it's hard
And hoping when it's hard
Keeping the faith when it's hard
Being kind when it's hard
Helping when it's hard.
I'll keep going,
Even though it's hard.

ALS

Life is fragile.
Light as a feather,
Then heavy as a cinder block.
Breaking through the darkness
Is the hope that the breeze brings the
feather back.
The weightlessness
-the transient sweetness-
Life is so much more than the rocks we
carry,
The rocks thrown at us.
Death's best attempt to cloak us in regret
In sorrow
In despair
Is hardly comparable to our weakest day in
the light.

He lifted his breathing mask away from his
face and told me,
in a soft and quiet voice,
"I have hospice care now."
I have visited him only a dozen times
before this news.
It still hurts, though.
Life's fragility,
The brevity of human experience.
The inability to breathe.

He says,
"I'm okay, though. I'm mentally healthy.
I'm in no pain. I'm okay with things."
I look over at his wife,
His partner for over 64 years,
And she says nothing.
Every time I visit him,
I water all the plants in the house.
His wife has had these plants since 2004,
When they first moved to Florida.
Today was no different
But the plants are dying.
All I could think
As I pulled away the dried out, dead leaves
From each plant
Is "...even the plants are dying"
And there's not much I can do
To stop any of it
Except to bring water,
Bring my hope and the extent of my
understanding,
and pour.
Lift away the rocks,
Help him center himself along the breeze's
direction,
And help him move
Much like a feather
To Heavenly Light.

Music to My Ears

Waking from a restless slumber
Events unraveling before me
The music plays so perfectly
the background voice sounds like
a conducted array of hopeful
notes
being written
just for me.
I hear church bells
but all the steeples burn
and people are crying
and hope is a dying man
who whispers,
"Just one more melody."
He disappears and
the notes fade out.
Decrescendo.
I don't know if they will ever come back,
to start singing a new verse.
A verse that brings that cross
on the pinnacle
to the brink
of creation.

The music plays so perfectly
that I can hear
the church bells sing.

Routine Blues

There's a reason for some things,
A rhyme we pick up on while we drive to
work
Do the dishes
Take a shower
Fall asleep.
We don't even realize the magnitude of
this rhyme,
This tune that follows us about our day.
It's live. Real time. Happening NOW.
I forget that when I'm in the moment.
I'm rarely in the moment.
We don't realize it, this magic touch that
outlines our lives.
I don't know the lyrics or the beat.
I know it's there, though,
Waiting for me to recognize the tone, the
pitch.
I woke up today thinking of my own
Reason for living.
I haven't discovered it yet,
But I'll let you know when I do.
When I find that tune,
I'll sing it back to you.

Control What You Let Go

Particles the size of salt
Slip through my fingers.
The hourglass beckons.
The hands on the clock work counter-
intuitively.
We are crumbling.
I see you smile.
You tell me you love me,
Waves degrading the shore.
A conch shell held to my ear,
Forgetting the hollow hum in the deep
grooves
Of my memories
Urging me to add this moment to the
chorus.
The hands on the clock regain composure
and move,
Tick
Tick
Ticking away
At life's most precious, unexchangeable
currency.
I bargain with God,
Convinced I can control the hands that
made me.
I forget that we are crumbling.

I forget that the hourglass is not on our
side.
I forget that
I'm still here to forget.
I'm still here to realize
My small role,
Much like one particle in the handful of
sand
Slipping through my fingers.

The Law of Conservation of Energy

A foundational law in physics and chemistry is the Law of Conservation of Energy: Energy cannot be created or destroyed; it only changes form.
All of us are made of energy. I wrote a poem that explains this scientific law in terms of grieving the loss of a loved one. I hope you find as much solace in this law as I have.

Daunting dreams of loved ones passed,
Clenched jaw, clenched fists, heart held against the glass.
Shatter the translucent globe,
the music stops with ambient light
Exposing the secrets, they whispered sweetly in the ear.
Midnight, 2 am, coffee brews and blinds closed.
Touching the framed picture with gentle hands,
the fragility of life faced.
A single tear falls against the smile,
Separated by a thin sheet of glass
But also, by another dimension,
Immeasurable miles.
Transcendental, energy dismissed.

They think the picture memorializes the
last kiss.
Let me tell you this:
In the breeze, in the sunshine,
In the rain, in the moonlight.
In the trees, in the snow,
Through the roads traveled,
Wherever we go,
The loved ones who have passed
Are the ones who outlast.
Life's fragility has met its match,
By a single law regarding energy.
You'll doubt it,
But it's been proven to be…
True: energy is dispersed throughout
The earth loses nothing, not even a tear.
Everything is collected, every breath
transferred.
It's beautiful, really,
That our lives are conserved.
See, whenever someone leaves,
Their spirit and body thought gone,
They've really only transformed
Into a new form of life.
A different heartbeat, a different song.
They sing a different tune,
They share their warmth with me and you,
Their energy as present as ever before.

The track changed; the melody separated
from this realm's shore.
Energy changes, but it cannot be created
or destroyed.
This means there should not be a void.
Our hearts ache and grieve because we
cannot grasp this concept
That our loved ones never left.
They have only changed form.
So, the next time you feel forlorn and
grieving,
Remember that they won't ever be
leaving.
The breaths you take,
The thoughts you create.
Our lives run on the energy,
blessed by our ancestors,
turning air into being.

Just Give Me A Reason

The ripple of a stone tossed
in water, dark and deep,
Moves still the feelings in my chest,
the beat that combs the streets.
For time has left my heart estranged,
By family, friend, and foe,
My eyes hold dear the meaningless,
Dreams deferred just so.
I walk; I breathe; I know the call
That brings me to my knees.
The depths that make my fingers curl into
a fist,
They blur my vision, salted sea.
I hear the echo of the righteous screams,
Declaring I've faced exile,
I walk; I breathe; I know the fall so well,
The feet becoming miles.
Starved for hope and open to change,
I see the face looking upon my choices.
The countenance transforms
Followed by a chorus of bellowing voices:
"Fear not, lest dreams become dismay
For when you move forward and find the
treasures lain
Ahead in your path and free to the one
who holds them first,
You will understand the process that

Gives your aspirations worth."
I struggle to open my eyes to see the
brightest Sun.
He smiles and carries me through the
chaos,
Oxygen in my lungs.
I don't walk; I run,
Defeat becoming ground.
My foundation was built with pain and loss.
In my painful moments, I have found:
The darkness passes and my vision
returns.
I can feed the fire and let it all burn,
Or hydrate the buds in my room,
So, they can grow, and they can bloom.
Life is so hard, unfair, and cruel.
Most days, I don't know how much living
we really do.
I reckon we all carry with us
Trials that never faced a jury.
You may be like me,
Feeling overwhelmed and hurried.
May we all find, before our deaths,
The courage to live a life that gives
Perpetual breaths
To those weary and tired, just like us.
We will realize none are exempt.
Some of us don't make it.
Some of us walk with a limp.

I run and I run,
Tired as I may be.
I don't want to give up.
I just want to be free.
You, with your busy, busy life
Can forget about me.
You judge. You disregard. You don't stop
to see...
You and I are participants in a race
In which no one ever wins.
All we can do is limit
The number of our sins.
All the while living as though our lives will
never end.
I just hope,
My mind will mend.
I hope to better understand the process
That gives my aspirations worth.
I hope our minds are healthy
When re-birthed.
I walk again; I breathe in deep,
I've more feet to become miles before I
sleep.
I walk, then pause,
To stare at the path before me.
I weep.
I walk; I breathe.
I pray to remember the good moments
I've felt,

Before I leap.
Turn back, turn away, and carry on.
Soon, you'll witness a brand-new dawn
to hold your fragile thoughts together,
So, you can survive any weather.
The question I ask of you isn't to know
your journey's length.
The question I ask pertains to your
strength.
I walk; I run; I stop to look at you, and
ask,
"If your scars were as visible as mine,
What kind of person would be unmasked?"
I show you my flesh,
My defeats revealed.
I resume walking,
We stop again at an open field.
What I want you to know
Is how far I will go to feel purpose.
I need to hear that the process is worth it.
Once we see through each other's eyes,
The catalyst of hate's demise,
We will find the walk, the run, the pause
Give meaning to connection and give hope
a cause.
Shall we all fight with every breath we
take.
God only knows what we can create.
I walk; I breathe; I pray for rest.

Until then, I pray, I'll do my best.
To tomorrow, to the future, to the past,
To now,
Give me a reason to keep going.
I'll survive any how.

Social Work
&
Advocacy

Eye Contact

I watch the homeless woman
selling newspapers on the roadside.
I've seen her standing there for two weeks
now
in 20-degree weather.
She has a warm smile.
No name
But plenty of shame
For being in that circumstance.
The shame is mine
for giving her quarters because I don't
have a dollar.
She smiles and says, "This is better. I need
quarters for bus money."
The shame is mine, really
because that could be any of us.
I usually avoid eye contact.
There was a war veteran on 4th avenue a
couple months ago.
He banged on a man's car window; every
inch of his body wracked with grief
of how "I was willing to die for you! You
won't even fucking look at me!"
of how he came back a broken man with a
fragmented mind.
How no one cares.
I usually avoid eye contact.

I usually don't see
the person on the street
as a person struggling to break free,
but as someone wallowing in their self-
pity.
I usually avoid eye contact.
But I didn't with the man on 4th avenue.
I could feel his agony.
I could feel his grief.
His heart is as big as the woman in 20-
degree weather.
But
People usually avoid eye contact.

I can't help but wonder...

Flipping through the channels on the tv,
I can't help wondering if we are all trapped
in the sea.
Trending and breaking news on the Web,
I can't help wondering if we don't have
any hope left.

I'm seeing stories of murder and rape.
I can't help wondering if Evil's disguised in
a hero's cape.
I'm hearing such harsh judgments and lack
of empathy.
I can't help wondering if our hearts are
experiencing entropy.

Humanity dwindling into chaos.
I can't help wondering if our compassion is
lost.

All the trees shading us are breaking.
Bombs and guns and violence berating
Kindness's gestures.
This world is reckless.
We are reckless.
We carry with us
Everything we need to succeed and love
But

We also carry with us
Everything we need to cause serious harm.

We have lost our sight.
There aren't any more rose-colored
glasses.
There isn't any more water to quench this
thirst
We all have.
We all need it; we must make a stand.
The dam is useless.
The barricades block nothing but more
drought.
I've been trying to build my house
Directly under the breaking trees
Right across the driest, hottest place.
I'm begging for those grey clouds.
No one's recognized my face.

They carry their guns,
And they use their words as venom.
They lurk in the shadows.
They shake my father's hand.
They hug you, then they gut you.
We must make a stand.

They are us; we are them
All of us walking on the same bridge,
The weight of us all pushing it to crumble.

I see how broken we all are,
How devoid we are of the humble
Yet resounding
Belief that
WE ARE ALL IN THIS TOGETHER.

We all have issues,
And we ~~don't~~ shouldn't need another crime
to see that.
The Light in me is searching for the
demons in you.
Feed the Good Wolf.
Don't let your doubts become true.
Anchor your feet in forgiveness and peace.
God knows we are all drowning in this sea.
We all need redemption and mercy.

For the people I've hurt,
For the people who've hurt me:
Patch the wounds,
Reclaim the cape.
This gaping wound in humanity is getting
bigger
Because of all this hate, I figure.
Hate won't drive out hate.
My heart grapples with life's fragility.
I know I'll try to increase the peace,
Even if it kills me.

The violence will hopefully cease,
I'm not sure when.
God knows we all need peace.
Until then, no one wins.
(No one's winning.)

If I had my life to live over

My present life looks a lot like it did two
years ago.
I'm living with my parents,
I go to the same university,
My best friend is 60 years my senior, and
I am not in a relationship.

On the outside looking in,
One might say my life hasn't really
changed that much.
But I moved out of my parent's house,
Earned my bachelor's degree and began
graduate school,
Strengthened my bond with my best
friend,
And started and ended a relationship
In the last two years.

My grandmother passed away last
November,
A month that's seen so many births in my
family.
But I know my mother wears her grief
Like a heavy cloak at the peak of summer
heat.

I now know what it is like to be a parent.

My little boy's smile wins my heart every
time.
He might be leaving my home in the next
month,
To live with his grandparents.
But he will never leave my heart.

We are so much more than the sum of our
parts.
Our lives transform by the spaces in
between
--the quiet introspection and lessons
learned—
The time will pass regardless.
The ebb and flow of gaining and losing,
Giving and taking,
The stopping and the going.

The only thing we truly carry through this
life
Is the reminder that we carry nothing at
all.
The direction my life is headed looks a lot
like yours,
And be it in sadness or joy,
In riches or rags,
In the quiet or the noise,
We are all just walking each other home.

In a Poor Man's Car

There sat a man,
Well groomed,
Light blue dress shirt with a tie,
A smile with eyes gleaming
A future full of promise
in a dirty
small
beat up
red coupe
on I-4.
I smiled, thinking
"What's on the inside doesn't always
match what's on the outside."
Was he on his way to a job interview?
Did his wife borrow "the good car"?
Was he a pastor on his way to a home
visit?
Was this man someone who saw the dirty
side of a dollar,
someone who knew the elbow grease and
sweat it took to feed a family?
Did this man love a lot of people and run
out of enough cash to get himself a
decent-looking car?
Or was this guy so focused on appearance
that he didn't have enough money for a
better car after

buying expensive hair products and suits?
We have this image of a man of faith,
one who always appears down on his luck
but he has infinite joy in his heart.
I wanted to know this guy's story,
the dirty car passing me on the interstate,
a face with seemingly no care in the world.
Pure bliss.
I thought,
"What a life he must lead
to not worry about whether his car will
make it,
to only care about the reflection in the
mirror."
I smiled,
simply by seeing a man who obviously has
a story
of whom I know nothing about
smiling so genuinely,
Like a rich man would

but he was alone
in a poor man's car.

Puzzle Pieces

If you've got a little more fight left in you,
now's the time to use it.
See, we've all got these pieces that don't
make sense.
Some of us questions it; others ask God
for hints
as to how our breaths will add up into a
perfectly wrapped purpose.
Some of us ask, "How is all this pain worth
it?"

Some of us use greed as fuel
and eat envy for breakfast.
But that money in your bank account will
not make your happiness last.
We all get caught up in the technicalities
in the idiosyncrasies
in the white noise
in the static.
I've forgotten that our brains are like
attics.

If you don't show yourself love,
If you don't give,
then your brain collects dust,
and your dreams turn to rust.
Everything ages.

Some of us have water leaks,
and some of us have thin white sheets
keeping everything neat.
"If I protect it, I won't lose it," we think.
In reality,
our brains need nourishment
and encouragement
and constant maintenance and
management.

Your attic may look like mine.
Mine has a very small window
that I open from time to time.
But mostly, it's closed and covered,
and my thoughts are never recovered.
We've all got our battles
and we've all got our memories.
We can't forget to care for our minds,
our personal attics.
We can't just avoid struggle.
We can't keep living through the static.
The attic is where we all find peace,
our minds like hands holding tight to
Hope.
You've already got that piece you've been
looking for
to make sense of it all.
Clean up your attic:
Repair the ceiling.

Throw away the sheets.
Use what you've been given,
for your mind is where
those pieces meet.

Someone Else

Have you ever thought about how the one
you love is disliked
by someone else,
How the person you dislike is someone
loved by someone else?
Have you ever thought about why?
What makes that person unlikeable?
What makes that same person lovable?
We all have pieces
Uncovered by someone else,
Each sliver of personality resonating within
someone.
We create questions,
But we also bring answers.
Namaste means, "the god in me respects
the god in you."
I think that's beautiful.
But
We must realize that our singular and very
personal battles culminate into
civil unrest
violence
catastrophe
war.
We forget that the person we don't like
was once an innocent infant,
is someone loved by God,

Is someone who exists for a purpose as
meaningful as our own.
We lose unconditional positive regard when
we forget the other person's life is also full
of
fears
and trials
and errors
and laughter
and pain
and questions needing to be answered.
I'm not saying we should play God,
But maybe the parts I dislike in others
Remind me of the parts I dislike in myself.
My body is my temple,
my vessel.
My feet support my travels,
My steep mountain climbs
and my graceless falls in the valley.
It is through redemption,
through loving someone else,
that I've begun to love myself.
It is through the giving,
through the mercy in my heart and the
effort to understand,
that I can find the good inside
someone else.
This life is made of struggle
after struggle

after struggle.
I can so easily forget that you are a lot like me
in our disagreements
and our opposing beliefs
and our inner voices both desperate to be heard.
We forget.
We forget that the ones we love are the same people others despise.
We forget that the ones we despise are the same people others love.
We just say, "You've got the wrong person. You must be referring to someone else..."
But no.
We forget that we are that "someone else."
Us.
The light to fight darkness,
The love to overcome hate,
The peace to combat violence,
The heart.
The heart,
It's always your heart.
My heart.
Our hearts beating, every breath leading us into understanding, compassion, and empathy.

If only we could remember more easily
than we forget:
we belong to each other.
We are on the same side,
the same team,
neither of us meant to last as
someone else.

Where are you, Jesus?

And the bombs detonate
And the tears fall
And the stars burst
And the cuffs are empty
And the people fall down
And the prisons are filled
But the peace can't be found.
And the children cry
And the good men die
And the smoke won't lift
And the skies won't clear
And the arctic ice melts
And nothing gives.
Crying for humanity
-the lack of humanity-
The bough is broken
Her huddled masses exiled
Sent back to the abyss
Degraded, defiled.

Jesus,
Where is the hope?
Where is the peace?
Where is my strength,
Everything good in me?
For this world devours itself,
Everyone is fighting with fire.

All I've got in my hands
Is this burning desire...
To see the rose attached to the thorny
stem,
To breathe easy, no "us versus them."
To feel the peace, the purpose behind
chaos.
To find a middle ground before all sight is
lost.
This humanity,
This uneven war,
The picking sides,
The endless lies,
The burying truth,
The dark grey skies.
The meaning behind the loss of hope,
Of life,
It's got to be found in You.
Isn't that right?

I've been fighting myself for far too long,
When I should have been fighting this
endless throng
Of injustice, of disharmony, of one-sided
respect.
My bruised knees and bloodied knuckles,
Praying night and day.
I'm one
-I'm someone-

I'm part of humanity.
Fighting against calamity,
The catalyst for peace.

Tears dry, smoke clears,
A message for you and me.
Eyes focused, vision strong.
The peace we've been searching for
Has been with us all along.

In Her Shoes

Driving past empty buildings,
Clock expresses night.
The glare from the windshield
Of passing cars' headlights.

We are talking about feelings,
Her face stiff and unkind.
I'd always thought her unfair,
Love costing quite a dime.

We are talking about telling people
they are loved.
She tells me how she was raised,
And I reply, "that sounds so rough."
We sit in silence as she drives,
The darkness feeding my curiosity.
I shift in the passenger seat,
My question leaving me:

"Since we are talking
About feelings and family,
I've been wondering why you never say
'I love you' to anyone."
She replied,
"I don't like who I've become."

She paused for a moment, then regained
her train of thought:
"I guess it's because my mom never said
it.
I never heard it. That hurt a lot."
She told me how she'd always planned to
be a mom who
Always told her children and family
"I love you."
After her candid answer,
We sat in silence a while longer.
She parked the car.
We'd arrived at the hospital
where her son was a patient.

An hour later, before she left his bedside,
I heard her say "I love you" to him,
Then she returned into the night.

Curtains and Streetlights

How do you know the right time to quit
when you've grown accustomed to losing?
And then you remember
moments when the curtains have been
drawn, but
the sun still finds its way through.
Nights when the moon can shine
brighter than all the
streetlights.
You see these moments
And you know
I know
That you never really lose.
We grow most from the experiences
We endure
and endure we must
To learn that
We never quit even after
the last breath we expel.
I hope I whisper,
"Open the curtains
Be the moon"
The brightest light in the room
Is always the one who must break through
It exposes everything much too soon
It beats what light was fastest of them all
To the finish line.

I want to see the finish line.
I want to run past all the ribbon
I'll see you on the other side of the
thought of
Quitting.
It's such a fickle belief.
Yet... choose wisely.
For some reason,
It can be the most liberating
or most catastrophic event

we must endure.

In Hiding

You have written the perfect monologue.
Your soliloquy in a sea of jumbled
nonsense.
You realize your words fall to deaf ears.
You step back and reevaluate your
wrongdoings.
Your steps backward,
Your mask behind a curtain.
How redundant the hiding is.
You notice a familiar voice.
He says he's been listening.
He takes his mask off.
You take yours off, too.

About the Author

Karah is a sexual violence survivor who received her master's degree in social work in 2021. She aspires to write and share poems that promote social justice, including gender and health equity. Karah believes in each person's potential to positively change and the healing power of writing to process grief and trauma. In her free time, you can find her playing with her two dogs, spending time with family, and volunteering in her community.